LIFE'S MOST EMBARRASSING MOMENTS

BY
STEVE
``MR. EMBARRASSMENT''
BERMAN

Illustrated by Don Smith

Those embarrassing and awkward situations we all get into that make us want to hide our heads in shame. How big a klutz are you compared to others? Take the quiz inside this book and find out. You'll have lots of fun playing along, and don't be surprised if your final score shocks the hell out of you!

CCC Publications • Los Angeles

Published by

CCC Publications
21630 Lassen St.
Chatsworth, CA 91311

Manufactured in the United States Of America

Cover © 1992 CCC Publications

Interior Illustrations © 1992 CCC Publications

Cover art by Don Smith

Interior art by Don Smith

Interior layout & production by Tim Bean/
DMC Publishing Group

ISBN: 0-918259-49-5

If your local U.S. bookstore is out of stock, copies of this book
may be obtained by mailing check or money order for $4.95 per
book (plus $2.50 to cover postage and handling) to:
CCC Publications; 21630 Lassen St. Chatsworth, CA 91311.

Pre-publication Edition - 2/93

ACKNOWLEDGEMENTS

First, there's Joseph Ross, who caught me walking out of the men's room at work one day with a long, white tail. He noticed that a piece of toilet paper had gotten caught in the back of my pants and was hanging down more than a foot. It was a tail that Peter Rabbit would be proud of (because female rabbits would consider him well hung), but for me it was an Embarrassing Moment. I've lived through worse Embarrassing Moments, but this embarrassing situation was special. It reminded me of other embarrassing episodes in my life, and I suddenly got the idea to write this book. So my warmest thanks to you, Joseph Ross, and to the White Cloud Toilet Paper Company, for their assistance. By the way, the commercials are right - White Cloud is the softest toilet paper around.

My deepest thanks to my dear friend, Elsie Schuller, for her undying support and top-notch secretarial skills.

Thanks also to Stephen Left, Jesse Ashby, Eileen Jackrel, Jeff Bale, Stacy and Wayne Farenga, and all the other idiots I know who offered encouragement and gave me great ideas while I was writing this book.

Special thanks to my exceptionally talented illustrator, Don Smith, who brought my zany ideas to life, and to my editor, Cliff Carle, and my publisher, Mark Chutick, for bringing this book to life.

And finally, thanks to all of mankind. If it weren't for all of you jerks out there who make embarrassing asses out of yourselves every day of the year like I do, I wouldn't have had the subject matter to write this book. Keep up the good work, you klutzes.

INTRODUCTION

We've all experienced real embarrassing situations that we'd rather forget about. When they occur, we usually feel like hiding in the closet and never coming out. But years later, we'll look back upon these incidents and laugh.

For example, have you ever:

- been caught with a big booger hanging out of your nose?

or

- been out in public and a bird craps on your head?

or

- farted loudly in a crowded room?

These are just a handful of the most embarrassing situations we all experience in life. There are many more as you'll soon see. When it happens you you it's not so funny, but when it happens to someone else, it can be a real belly-laugh. Therefore, a WARNING. It has been reported that some people who have read this book have laughed so hard that they've fractured jaw bones or popped blood vessels. Some readers have even developed chronic cases of non-stop hiccups. So if you're insured, read on!

HOW TO USE THIS BOOK

Listed in this book are numerous examples of Life's Most Embarrassing Moments. How do you compare to others when it comes to getting yourself into situations that cause you to turn beet red? Well, now you can find out, and discover for yourself whether you're really cool or a big klutz.

To learn how you measure up, here's what you do:

1. Grab a pencil or pen.

2. As you read the embarrassing situations, you'll see a box at the bottom of the page labeled "EMBARRASSMENT LEVEL". If you've ever experienced an embarrassing moment **similar to the situation** being described, you'll be instructed to enter a number between one and six depending on the degree of embarrassment.

3. After you've finished, go back and count up the total number of points to arrive at your score.

4. Finally, look at the page at the end of the book entitled "Tallying Your Score" to find out if, in fact, you really are a big klutz and didn't know it.

5. For party fun, try to be honest when scoring and compare your total with your friends'.

WHILE IN BED MAKING LOVE, YOUR KID UNEXPECTEDLY WALKED INTO THE ROOM.

EMBARRASSMENT LEVEL: 4 POINTS.

AT A PARTY, THE HOST'S DOG STARTED HUMPING YOUR LEG.

EMBARRASSMENT LEVEL:
3 POINTS.

YOU CAME OUT OF THE SHOWER AND NOTICED THE SHADES WERE UP. AS YOU WENT TO CLOSE THEM, A NEIGHBOR SAW YOU.

EMBARRASSMENT LEVEL: 5 POINTS.

YOU FORGOT TO FLUSH THE TOILET AND COMPANY ARRIVED.

☐ EMBARRASSMENT LEVEL:
6 POINTS.

WHILE DRIVING, ONE OF YOUR HUBCAPS FELL OFF AND HIT THE CAR NEXT TO YOU.

☐ EMBARRASSMENT LEVEL:
2 POINTS.

YOU CUT YOURSELF BADLY WHILE SHAVING, AND WERE FORCED TO GO TO WORK WITH A FACE FULL OF BANDAGES, LOOKING LIKE A MUMMY.

☐ EMBARRASSMENT LEVEL:
2 POINTS.

YOU CALLED YOUR GIRLFRIEND AND SAID INTIMATE THINGS. YOU SOON DISCOVERED YOU DIALED THE WRONG NUMBER.

HELLO, POOPSIE, THIS IS YOUR LITTLE ALL DAY SUCKER... I'M COMIN' OVER AND LET YOU LICK ME ALL OVER.

EMBARRASSMENT LEVEL: 3 POINTS.

YOU SHOWED UP AT A PARTY OVERDRESSED.

EMBARRASSMENT LEVEL:
3 POINTS.

WHEN YOU RETURNED FROM LUNCH, YOU SMILED AT A CO-WORKER, AND SHE NOTICED YOU HAD FOOD STUCK IN YOUR TEETH.

EMBARRASSMENT LEVEL: 3 POINTS.

YOU ACCIDENTLY HONKED YOUR HORN AT THE DRIVER IN FRONT OF YOU AND HE GAVE YOU THE FINGER.

☐ EMBARRASSMENT LEVEL:
2 POINTS.

WHILE OUT ON A DATE IN YOUR SHINY NEW SPORTS CAR WITH A GIRL YOU REALLY WANTED TO IMPRESS, THE CAR BROKE DOWN.

☐ EMBARRASSMENT LEVEL:
3 POINTS.

YOU WERE SITTING ON THE TOILET AT A PARTY, AND SOMEONE WALKED IN.

☐ EMBARRASSMENT LEVEL:
4 POINTS.

YOU GOT CAUGHT MAKING NOISY LOVE.

EMBARRASSMENT LEVEL:
4 POINTS.

YOU YELLED OUT "BINGO" BY MISTAKE.

EMBARRASSMENT LEVEL:
1 POINT.

IN THE MIDDLE OF A SPEECH, YOU DISCOVERED THERE WAS A BAD RUN IN YOUR PANTYHOSE.

EMBARRASSMENT LEVEL:
3 POINTS.

YOUR BLIND DATE TURNED OUT TO BE A REAL DOG AND YOU DESPERATELY TRIED TO GET OUT OF IT.

EMBARRASSMENT LEVEL:
3 POINTS.

YOU WERE CAUGHT LISTENING TO A PRIVATE CONVERSATION.

☐ EMBARRASSMENT LEVEL:
3 POINTS.

THE DRIVER KICKED YOU OFF THE BUS FOR NOT HAVING THE EXACT CHANGE.

☐ EMBARRASSMENT LEVEL:
1 POINT.

AFTER A DAY OUT IN PUBLIC, YOU LOOKED IN A MIRROR AND NOTICED THAT YOU HAD A LONG, UGLY NOSE HAIR HANGING OUT.

☐ EMBARRASSMENT LEVEL:
2 POINTS.

YOUR CHILD MADE YOU LOOK LIKE A FOOL WHEN SHE REPEATED SOMETHING SHE HEARD YOU SAY.

EMBARRASSMENT LEVEL:
6 POINTS.

YOUR NEIGHBOR ANGRILY INFORMED YOU THAT YOUR DOG POOPED ON HIS LAWN AGAIN.

EMBARRASSMENT LEVEL:
2 POINTS.

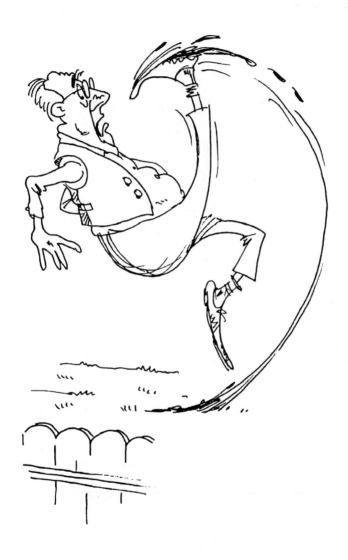

YOU CAME OUT OF THE MEN'S ROOM, FORGOT TO ZIP YOUR FLY, AND DIDN'T REALIZE IT UNTIL TWO HOURS LATER.

EMBARRASSMENT LEVEL: 3 POINTS.

YOU FORGOT WHAT YOUR YOUR MOTHER ALWAYS SAID ABOUT CHECKING YOUR UNDERWEAR TO MAKE SURE THEY WERE CLEAN BEFORE GOING TO THE DOCTOR.

EMBARRASSMENT LEVEL:
4 POINTS.

YOU WERE AT A FORMAL AFFAIR. PEOPLE STARTED STARING AT YOU. YOU THOUGHT IT WAS BECAUSE YOU LOOKED BEAUTIFUL IN YOUR NEW DRESS, BUT LATER YOU REALIZED YOUR SLIP WAS SHOWING A FULL SIX INCHES.

☐ EMBARRASSMENT LEVEL: 3 POINTS.

JUST AS YOU WERE PURCHASING A BOX OF CONDOMS, A CROWD OF PEOPLE ARRIVED AT THE CHECKOUT COUNTER.

☐ EMBARRASSMENT LEVEL: 3 POINTS.

YOUR PANTYHOSE GOT STUCK IN YOUR SKIRT. YOU TRID TO FIX THE PROBLEM, AND PEOPLE SAW YOU PULLING AT YOUR CROTCH.

☐ EMBARRASSMENT LEVEL: 2 POINTS.

YOU WERE RUDELY SHOT DOWN FOR A DATE AND YOUR FRIEND SAW IT HAPPEN.

EMBARRASSMENT LEVEL:
3 POINTS.

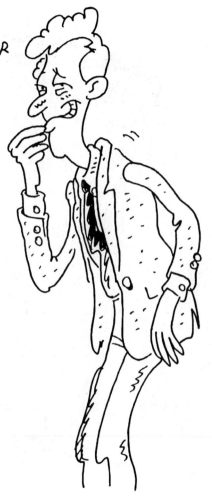

IN A CROWDED ROOM, YOU ACCIDENTLY LET OUT A LOUD ONE AND EVERYONE KNEW IT WAS YOU.

EMBARRASSMENT LEVEL: 6 POINTS.

PEOPLE THREW YOU DIRTY LOOKS AS YOU EXITED THE BATHROOM WITHOUT WASHING YOUR HANDS.

EMBARRASSMENT LEVEL:
3 POINTS.

IT WAS THE LAST INNING OF THE GAME. YOUR TEAM WAS BEHIND BY ONE RUN. THE BASES WERE LOADED, AND YOUR TEAM HAD TWO OUTS. IT WAS ALL UP TO YOU, AND YOU STRUCK OUT.

EMBARRASSMENT LEVEL:
3 POINTS.

AT A CAFETERIA YOU ACCIDENTALLY SPILLED A CUP OF HOT COFFEE ON THE PEOPLE SITTING NEAR YOU.

EMBARRASSMENT LEVEL:
3 POINTS.

SOMEONE READ YOUR DIARY.

EMBARRASSMENT LEVEL:
3 POINTS.

YOU WERE BRAGGING TO YOUR PASSENGERS ABOUT WHAT A GOOD DRIVER YOU ARE, AND SUDDENLY DISCOVERED YOU WERE GOING THE WRONG WAY ON A ONE-WAY STREET.

☐ EMBARRASSMENT LEVEL:
3 POINTS.

AFTER FALLING OFF YOUR DIET, YOU WERE OUT IN PUBLIC AND DISCOVERED YOUR SHIRT DIDN'T QUITE COVER YOUR ENTIRE STOMACH.

☐ EMBARRASSMENT LEVEL:
2 POINTS.

YOU SHOWED UP AT AN IMPORTANT ENGAGEMENT, REALIZED YOU FORGOT TO SHAVE, AND LOOK LIKE A BUM.

☐ EMBARRASSMENT LEVEL:
3 POINTS.

YOU ACCIDENTALLY WENT TO THE WRONG WAKE.

EMBARRASSMENT LEVEL:
3 POINTS.

IF YOU'RE LOOKING FOR MR. SMEDLEY, MADAM, I BELIEVE THAT'S HIM YOU'RE USING FOR AN ASHTRAY.

YOU SNEEZED IN A CROWDED ELEVATOR.

EMBARRASSMENT LEVEL:
3 POINTS.

THE ONE TIME YOU FORGOT TO PUT TAMPONS IN YOUR PURSE, YOU GOT YOUR PERIOD.

☐ EMBARRASSMENT LEVEL:
4 POINTS.

YOU ARRIVED AT A PARTY TOO EARLY, AND HAD TO HANG AROUND, LOOKING LIKE A DESPERATE FOOL, UNTIL THE OTHER GUESTS ARRIVED.

☐ EMBARRASSMENT LEVEL:
2 POINTS.

YOU ARRIVED LATE TO AN IMPORTANT BUSINESS MEETING, AND MADE UP A DUMB-ASS EXCUSE THAT YOU KNEW NOBODY BELIEVED.

☐ EMBARRASSMENT LEVEL:
3 POINTS.

YOU WERE IN A HURRY, NOT PAYING ATTENTION, AND ACCIDENTALLY WALKED INTO THE WRONG BATHROOM.

EMBARRASSMENT LEVEL:
3 POINTS.

YOU WERE IN BED WITH A BEAUTIFUL WOMAN. IT HAD BEEN A LONG NIGHT. YOU'D DRANK A LOT, WERE TIRED, AND COULDN'T PERFORM.

EMBARRASSMENT LEVEL:
5 POINTS.

YOU FORGOT TO CLEAN THE CAT LITTER AND COMPANY ARRIVED.

EMBARRASSMENT LEVEL:
3 POINTS.

AS THE SUPERMARKET CASHIER RANG UP YOUR GROCERIES, YOU REALIZED YOU DIDN'T HAVE ENOUGH MONEY TO PAY, AND HAD TO START SELECTING ITEMS TO GIVE BACK.

EMBARRASSMENT LEVEL: 3 POINTS.

YOUR NOSE WAS RUNNING, YOU DIDN'T HAVE A TISSUE AND YOU GOT CAUGHT USING YOUR SLEEVE.

EMBARRASSMENT LEVEL:
2 POINTS.

YOU WERE HAVING DINNER OUT WITH FRIENDS, AND ACCIDENTLLY SPILLED SOME OF YOUR DRINK IN YOUR CROTCH AREA. IF YOU STOOD UP, EVERYONE AROUND YOU WOULD THINK YOU MADE PEE-PEE IN YOUR PANTS.

EMBARRASSMENT LEVEL:
4 POINTS.

IN FRONT OF ALL YOUR CLASSMATES, THE TEACHER CAUGHT YOU CHEATING ON A HIGH SCHOOL EXAM.

EMBARRASSMENT LEVEL:
2 POINTS.

YOU WERE OUT IN PUBLIC WEARING A SEE-THROUGH BLOUSE, AND YOUR BRA UNSNAPED.

EMBARRASSMENT LEVEL:
2 POINTS.

YOU WERE SEEN ENTERING A DIRTY MOVIE THEATER.

EMBARRASSMENT LEVEL: 5 POINTS.

YOU GOT CAUGHT TALKING BEHIND SOMEONE'S BACK.

EMBARRASSMENT LEVEL:
4 POINTS.

YOU WERE STOPPED AT A RED LIGHT. YOU DIDN'T NOTICE THAT THE LIGHT TURNED GREEN AND CARS BEHIND YOU BEGAN TO HONK ANGRILY.

EMBARRASSMENT LEVEL: 2 POINTS.

YOU DIDN'T REALIZE UNTIL LATER THAT NIGHT THAT YOU HAD A BIG BOOGER HANGING OUT OF YOUR NOSE ALL DAY.

☐ EMBARRASSMENT LEVEL:
3 POINTS.

YOU WERE AT A PARTY TRYING TO ACT SOPHISTICATED, AND LIT THE WRONG END OF A CIGARETTE.

☐ EMBARRASSMENT LEVEL:
2 POINTS.

AT A DINNER PARTY, YOU'D JUST EATEN A BIG MEAL. AS YOU WERE TALKING TO THE OTHER GUESTS, YOU SUDDENLY, AND UNCONTROLLABLY, LET OUT A LOUD BELCH.

☐ EMBARRASSMENT LEVEL:
3 POINTS.

AS YOU WERE WALKING DOWN THE STREET, A GUST OF WIND BLEW YOUR DRESS UP.

EMBARRASSMENT LEVEL: 3 POINTS.

AT A FANCY RESTAURANT WITH YOUR DATE, THE WAITER ANNOUNCED THAT YOUR CREDIT CARD WAS REFUSED.

EMBARRASSMENT LEVEL: 5 POINTS.

YOU WERE CHEWING GUM AND TRYING TO ACT COOL IN FRONT OF A BUNCH OF YOUR FRIENDS. YOU BLEW A BIG BUBBLE THAT POPPED ALL OVER YOUR FACE.

☐ EMBARRASSMENT LEVEL:
2 POINTS.

YOU RAN INTO AN OLD FRIEND YOU HADN'T SEEN IN A WHILE. YOU CONGRATULATED HER ON HER PREGNANCY AND ASKED WHEN SHE WAS DUE. IT TURNED OUT SHE HAD JUST GAINED A LOT OF WEIGHT.

☐ EMBARRASSMENT LEVEL:
3 POINTS.

YOUR WIFE CAUGHT YOU FLIRTING WITH ANOTHER WOMAN.

☐ EMBARRASSMENT LEVEL:
2 POINTS.

YOU WERE CAUGHT SNORING LOUDLY DURING A SERMON.

EMBARRASSMENT LEVEL:
2 POINTS.

EARLY ONE MORNING YOU WERE STILL IN YOUR NIGHTGOWN. YOU TOOK OUT THE TRASH, AND REALIZED YOU LOCKED YOURSELF OUT OF THE HOUSE.

CLICK

EMBARRASSMENT LEVEL: 4 POINTS.

AT A BUSINESS MEETING YOU LEANED BACK IN YOUR CHAIR. IT TIPPED OVER AND YOU FELL FLAT ON YOUR ASS.

EMBARRASSMENT LEVEL:
3 POINTS.

YOU WANDERED AIMLESSLY AROUND A PARKING LOT, HAVING FORGOTTEN WHERE YOU PARKED YOUR CAR.

EMBARRASSMENT LEVEL:
2 POINTS.

YOU HAD A BAD CASE OF THE RUNS WHILE OUT WITH FRIENDS, AND YOU COULDN'T FIND A BATHROOM IN TIME.

EMBARRASSMENT LEVEL:
5 POINTS.

WHILE OUT FOR A MEAL YOU WERE TALKING WITH YOUR MOUTH FULL, AND ACCIDENTALLY SPIT FOOD IN SOMEONE'S FACE.

EMBARRASSMENT LEVEL:
3 POINTS.

YOU WALKED OUT OF THE BATHROOM AT WORK, UNAWARE AT FIRST, THAT YOU HAD TOILET PAPER HANGING OUT OF YOUR DRESS.

EMBARRASSMENT LEVEL:
3 POINTS.

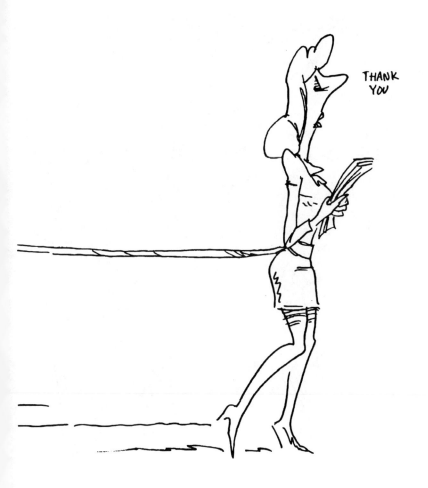

YOU RAN INTO SOME FRIENDS WHO LET YOU KNOW THAT YOUR BREATH STINKS.

EMBARRASSMENT LEVEL:
4 POINTS.

YOU WERE SEEN IN THE UNEMPLOYMENT LINE.

UNEMPLOYMENT
LINE

EMBARRASSMENT LEVEL:
3 POINTS.

IN THE MIDDLE OF A DREAM, YOU CALLED OUT A WOMAN'S NAME, BUT IT WAS <u>NOT</u> YOUR WIFE'S NAME.

EMBARRASSMENT LEVEL: 2 POINTS.

YOU COULDN'T STOP COUGHING IN A MOVIE THEATRE.

EMBARRASSMENT LEVEL:
2 POINTS.

YOU SMELLED UP THE BATHROOM AT A FRIEND'S HOUSE, SEARCHED DESPARATELY FOR A CAN OF AIR FRESHENER, BUT THERE WAS NONE. THEN SUDDENLY, THERE WAS A KNOCK AT THE DOOR.

EMBARRASSMENT LEVEL:
4 POINTS.

WHILE SWIMMING AT A CROWDED BEACH, A LARGE WAVE KNOCKED YOU OVER AND YOUR BATHING SUIT FELL OFF.

EMBARRASSMENT LEVEL: 5 POINTS.

YOU WORE A TINY BIKINI TO A PUBLIC BEACH AND FORGOT TO TRIM YOUR PRIVATE AREA.

☐ EMBARRASSMENT LEVEL:
5 POINTS.

A COP STOPPED YOU, AND WHILE HE WAS GIVING YOU A TICKET, SEVERAL OF YOUR FRIENDS DROVE BY.

☐ EMBARRASSMENT LEVEL:
2 POINTS.

WHILE VISITING FRIENDS YOU ACCIDENTALLY BURNED A BIG HOLE IN THEIR NEW CARPET WITH YOUR CIGARETTE.

☐ EMBARRASSMENT LEVEL:
2 POINTS.

A COP CAUGHT YOU MAKING OUT WITH YOUR GIRLFRIEND.

EMBARRASSMENT LEVEL:
2 POINTS.

YOUR WIFE CAUGHT YOU READING A "DIRTY" MAGAZINE.

EMBARRASSMENT LEVEL:
2 POINTS.

YOU GOT FIRED FROM YOUR JOB IN FRONT OF YOUR COWORKERS.

EMBARRASSMENT LEVEL:
6 POINTS.

YOU SAW SOMEONE YOU THOUGHT YOU KNEW, BUT IT TURNED OUT TO BE THE WRONG PERSON.

EMBARRASSMENT LEVEL:
3 POINTS.

OOOOH! I'D LOVE TO BE YOUR BABYKINS!
AND YOU CAN BE MY BIG TEDDY BEAR.

YOUR WIFE SENT YOU OUT TO BUY SANITARY NAPKINS.

EMBARRASSMENT LEVEL:
4 POINTS.

YOU GOT A BOTCHED-UP HAIRCUT THAT MADE YOU LOOK LIKE A FREAK, AND YOU WERE AFRAID TO BE SEEN IN PUBLIC.

☐ EMBARRASSMENT LEVEL:
3 POINTS.

YOUR BABY SPIT UP ALL OVER A STRANGER.

☐ EMBARRASSMENT LEVEL:
3 POINTS.

YOU GOT CAUGHT LIGHTING-UP IN A NON-SMOKING AREA AND WERE GIVEN A STERN LECTURE.

☐ EMBARRASSMENT LEVEL:
1 POINT.

A CO-WORKER DROPPED A NOTEPAD. YOU CHIVALROUSLY BENT DOWN TO PICK IT UP AND SPLIT THE SEAM IN THE SEAT OF YOUR PANTS.

EMBARRASSMENT LEVEL:
4 POINTS.

YOU ANGRILY CUT SOMEONE OFF THE ROAD WHILE DRIVING, AND IT TURNED OUT TO BE SOMEONE YOU KNOW.

☐ EMBARRASSMENT LEVEL:
3 POINTS.

YOU GOT SEASICK, AND PUKED YOUR GUTS UP IN FRONT OF PEOPLE.

☐ EMBARRASSMENT LEVEL:
6 POINTS.

YOU FELT LIKE A REAL LOONEY WHEN YOU GOT CAUGHT TALKING TO YOURSELF.

☐ EMBARRASSMENT LEVEL:
2 POINTS.

A SUDDEN GUST OF WIND BLEW YOUR HAIRPIECE OFF.

EMBARRASSMENT LEVEL: 5 POINTS.

YOUR BOSS NEEDED A LIFT TO THE AIRPORT AND YOU VOLUNTEERED. WHEN YOU REACHED YOUR CAR, YOU REALIZED YOU LOCKED YOUR KEYS INSIDE.

EMBARRASSMENT LEVEL: 3 POINTS.

WHILE ASLEEP OR DAY-DREAMING IN CLASS THE TEACHER CALLED ON YOU TO ANSWER A QUESTION.

☐ EMBARRASSMENT LEVEL:
2 POINTS.

YOU WERE HURRYING DOWN A FLIGHT OF STAIRS, YOU TRIPPED AND FELL ON PEOPLE.

☐ EMBARRASSMENT LEVEL:
3 POINTS.

WHILE ON A DATE WITH A PERSON YOU REALLY LIKED, YOUR SCOOP OF ICE CREAM FELL OFF YOUR CONE AND DRIBBLED ALL OVER YOU.

☐ EMBARRASSMENT LEVEL:
2 POINTS.

EMBARRASSMENT LEVEL: 2 POINTS.

YOU DIDN'T REALIZE UNTIL YOU REACHED THE OFFICE THAT YOU HAD ACCIDENTALLY PUT ON DIFFERENT COLOR SOCKS.

EMBARRASSMENT LEVEL: 1 POINT.

SOMEONE YOU KNEW WALKED UP AND GREETED YOU BY NAME. YOU FELT LIKE AN ASS WHEN YOU COULDN'T REMEMBER HIS NAME.

EMBARRASSMENT LEVEL:
4 POINTS.

WHEN WALKING IN PUBLIC, A BIRD CRAPPED ON YOUR HEAD.

EMBARRASSMENT LEVEL: 5 POINTS.

YOU GOT CAUGHT ACCIDENTALLY TRYING TO OPEN THE DOOR OF A CAR THAT YOU MISTOOK FOR YOURS.

EMBARRASSMENT LEVEL:
2 POINTS.

YOUR FALSE TEETH FELL OUT WHILE EATING IN A RESTAURANT.

WHY, MR. ERDLAP,
SURELY YOU'VE
SEEN A DIAMOND
NECKLACE BEFORE

EMBARRASSMENT LEVEL:
3 POINTS.

IT WAS PROM NIGHT, AND JUST YOUR LUCK — YOU BROKE OUT WITH A GREAT BIG ZIT.

EMBARRASSMENT LEVEL:
4 POINTS.

YOU WERE STOPPED BY A SECURITY GUARD AND ACCUSED OF SHOPLIFTING BECAUSE THE SALES CLERK FORGOT TO REMOVE THE PLASTIC SECURITY CLIP ATTACHED TO THE DRESS YOU JUST PURCHASED.

EMBARRASSMENT LEVEL:
6 POINTS.

YOU GOT CAUGHT PICKING YOUR NOSE WHILE DRIVING IN YOUR CAR.

EMBARRASSMENT LEVEL:
4 POINTS.

95

YOU GOT CAUGHT SPYING ON A GIRL'S SLUMBER PARTY.

EMBARRASSMENT LEVEL:
2 POINTS.

YOU STEPPED IN A BIG PILE OF DOG DOODY WHILE OUT ON A DATE.

EMBARRASSMENT LEVEL:
3 POINTS.

YOU GOT DRUNK AT AN OFFICE PARTY AND MADE A FOOL OF YOURSELF. YOU REMEMBERED THE WHOLE THING WHEN YOU WOKE UP THE NEXT MORNING AND WERE AFRAID TO GO BACK TO WORK.

EMBARRASSMENT LEVEL:
5 POINTS.

YOU GOT CAUGHT IN A LIE.

I WAS LEAVING WORK WHEN–WHO
DO I RUN INTO BUT... UH... ELVIS.' YEAH,
IT WAS REALLY ELVIS! AND HE SAYS, 'HEY,
MARV, LET'S HAVE A COUPLE DRINKS DOWN
AT MOTEL 6.. IT'S JUST ME AND MARILYN.'..
AND THERE WAS MARILYN MONROE! I
COULDN'T BELIEVE MY EYES! WELL, MARILYN'S
ALL OVER ME! WE WERE IN THE BACK
SEAT OF JAMES DEAN'S PORSCHE.. YEAH..
JAMES DEAN.. AND THE NEXT THING
I KNOW WE'RE WITH THE....UH...
SWEDISH BIKINI TEAM.. AND

EMBARRASSMENT LEVEL:
3 POINTS.

YOU WERE IN A PUBLIC BATHROOM. WHEN YOU WERE DONE, YOU REALIZED THERE WAS NO TOILET PAPER.

EMBARRASSMENT LEVEL: 5 POINTS.

TALLYING YOUR SCORE

Okay, now it's time to add up the total number of points you've amassed. Next, look at the table below to find out how you rate as an embarrassment in life.

RATINGS

SCORE OF 251 - 325 ....You're a HOPLESS KLUTZ. Dig a hole and bury yourself.

SCORE OF 201 - 250 ....You're an INTERMEDIATE KLUTZ. In another year or two you'll become the complete klutz you were born to be.

SCORE OF 101 - 200 ....You're a BORDERLINE KLUTZ. You've been pretty lucky so far. But beware, your luck is bound to wear out, and you'll become as big of a klutz as everyone else.

SCORE OF 0 - 100 ....You're a DAMN LIAR. (no one scores this low!) You should be embarrassed! As a penalty add 300 points.

CONCLUSION

We're all human and we all experience embarrassing situations. So if you got a high score on the quiz, don't sweat it. You're in good company. Look at me, the author. I'm the biggest embarrassment going.

If you're still feeling bad about your score, though, you can do one of two things. You can take the quiz again, and this time, lie or you can pray that the next time an embarrassing situation occurs, you'll be witnessing it rather than experiencing it!

ABOUT THE AUTHOR

Steve Berman has worked as a writer for more than 20 years. He's authored several business books, and has written comedy material for film, television, newspapers and magazines.

Over the years, he's gotten himself into more embarrassing situations than Jehovah has witnesses. It's no wonder that those who know him refer to him affectionately as "Mr. Embarrassment." It's a nickname that he's had for many years, and will probably be forced to live with until he croaks. Once an ass, always an ass.

Originally from New York City, he now resides in North Miami Beach, Florida with all the other old people.

TITLES BY CCC PUBLICATIONS

— NEW BOOKS —

LIFE'S MOST EMBARRASSING MOMENTS..............$4.95

THE BOTTOM HALF..$4.95

HOW TO ENTERTAIN PEOPLE YOU HATE $4.95

NEVER A DULL CARD $5.95

WORK SUCKS!..$5.95

THE UGLY TRUTH ABOUT MEN $5.95

IT'S BETTER TO BE OVER THE HILL-
       THAN UNDER IT $5.95

THE PEOPLE WATCHER'S FIELD GUIDE................$5.95

THE GUILT BAG (Accessory Item)..........................$6.95

HOW TO REALLY PARTY..$5.95

THE ABSOLUTE **LAST CHANCE**
       DIET BOOK..$5.95

HUSBANDS FROM HELL..$5.95

HORMONES FROM HELL (The Ultimate
      Women's Humor Book!)...............................$5.95

FOR **MEN** ONLY (How To Survive Marriage) $5.95

THE Unofficial WOMEN'S DIVORCE GUIDE............$5.95

HOW TO TALK YOUR WAY OUT OF A
      TRAFFIC TICKET..$4.95

WHAT DO WE DO NOW?? (The Complete Guide
      For All New Parents) $4.95

— COMING SOON —

THE KNOW-IT-ALL HANDBOOK

— BEST SELLERS—

— CASSETTES —

5. Contest begins April 1, 1993. Entries must be postmarked by December 31, 1993. Winners will be selected on January 31, 1994 and notified by mail within 30 days.

6. Entry constitutes permission to use winners' names and likenesses for promotional purposes. Additionally, winners may be required to sign and return an affidavit of eligibility and a release within 30 days of notification for publicity purposes and without further compensation. Otherwise alternate winners may be selected.

7. Limit: one major prize per family or household. Employees of CCC Publications, their families, agencies and representatives are not eligible. No substitutions for prizes offered. Tax liability to be borne solely by the winners. Void where prohibited.

8. CCC Publications shall not be liable for late, misdirected, lost or stolen entries.

9. For a list of major prize winners, or for a copy of the official rules, send a <u>separate</u> stamped and self-addressed envelope to "America's Most Embarrassing Moments" Winners List -or- "America's Most Embarrassing Moments" Contest Rules; c/o CCC PUBLICATIONS; 21630 Lassen Street; Chatsworth, CA 91311.

10. In the event CCC Publications decides to use a non-winning "Most Embarrassing Moment," entry after contest closing in a future book, the entrant shall receive $5.00 and their name will appear in said book.

ALL MONEY PRIZES GUARANTEED TO BE AWARDED!!!